Light to Light

poems by

Kate McNairy

Finishing Line Press
Georgetown, Kentucky

Light to Light

Copyright © 2016 by Kate McNairy
ISBN 978-1-63534-073-0 First Edition
All rights reserved under International and Pan-American Copyright Conventions. No part of this book may be reproduced in any manner whatsoever without written permission from the publisher, except in the case of brief quotations embodied in critical articles and reviews.

ACKNOWLEDGMENTS

Thank you to the following periodicals for publishing poems included in this collection.

A Hudson View—"Wet Bodies"
Gnosis—"This is Probably True," "A Cup of Coffee," "Pool at 3:00 a.m."

Publisher: Leah Maines

Editor: Christen Kincaid

Cover Art: Victor Moscoso

Author Photo: Elizabeth Macy

Cover Design: Elizabeth Maines

Printed in the USA on acid-free paper.
Order online: www.finishinglinepress.com
also available on amazon.com

Author inquiries and mail orders:
Finishing Line Press
P. O. Box 1626
Georgetown, Kentucky 40324
U. S. A.

Table of Contents

A Cup of Coffee 1
Play 2
A Cup of Rum Tea 3
Bourbon 4
Tremor 5
Wet Bodies 6
Rub 7
Amuse 8
On the Roof 9
Rain 10
Into the Night 11
In the Pocket 12
Morning Rain 13
Comets 14
Mother 15
Pool at 3:00 a.m. 16
The Ride of Our Lives 17
So Right, So Wild 18
What Is 19
Candle 20
Tossed Aside 21
Storm 22
This Is Probably True 23
Returning 24
Armadillo 25
Night Stars 26

*For
Jon*

Arise from sleep, old cat,
and with great yawns
and stretchings ...
amble out for love

Issa

A Cup of Coffee

The neon lights
of a convenience store
beckon me—
some smokes,
a newspaper,
a cup of coffee.

No one is here.
I ring the bell
on the counter.
No one comes.

As I leave
with nothing,
I see snow
tumbling onto
streetlights,
houses, trees.

So many people
are eager to invite
me to their dwellings,
hunger to tell me
their stories.
Such is the way
with us, the lonely.

I toy with the idea
of a second life.
If I could,
my love,
I would gladly
begin again.

Play

Never trust the look
of love's debris.
By the time it is noticed
it has already happened.

Never trust love's reverse:
a tired brake,
a drunken steering column,
weeping wheels.

Love's magician pulls us from
his hat to earth's other side
where love, like white rabbits,
knows only innocence.

Do not count out our convoluted love.
We mourners wear its vestiges
as we rehearse the approach.
Love's play opens tonight.

A Cup of Rum Tea

The house is
so spare, so Zen.
Snowing
at twilight,
the flakes plump
and soft.

Gwen is here,
once more.

We have been
drinking
not just tea, but
dark, rum tea;
so quirky,
for us.

She pushed her
chair aside,
and left.

I thought,
she is walking
—how wonderful—
on a journey
around the
pond.

Her hat
and coat
lay abandoned.

Bourbon

Whether it is sun or moon,
I carry a candle, a light inside me.

My quiet chaos—
late night bourbon,
domestic quarrels,
kids gone awry.

I carry all this
mayhem inside me,
silently lit by the heat of the candle.

Tremor

Darkness covers
Long Island sound.
I hold my lover's hand
as we slant into the rain.
There is a tiny tremor in our hearts.

Our journey through weather;
electrons jump
in and out of their orbits.

What could be a worse storm—
emptiness that thinks it is something,
or the reverse?

Wet Bodies

Bring on the heat,
dark spots on the sun,
harsh, unforgiving.
The earth shifts and moves.
The oceans bubble over.
We wait until
the sun drops, our
temperatures rise, our
bodies wet and tangled.

We press on until dawn.

Rub

What is outer
is inner.
That's the rub
of this world.

I'm trying to
figure this out.

I dream
of you with
a smoldering cigarette
clouding the sky—
you, my capricious lover,
flying in the wind.

These words
rest in weeds
grown askew
in my dream.

However brief
they may live,
wake me
wake me.

Amuse

A myriad
of stars tethers
our bed
to skies.

We lie in
blue sheets,
fleshy skin—
tumbling to sleep.

You ask if
I am amused.

In an instant
my life, a string,
threads a needle
through
my optic nerve,
electrical, elliptical—

our bodies' desire,
our souls' ecstatic—
a cacophony.

Palm my eyes,
calm them.
Yes man,
I am amused,
yes, my man.

On the Roof

I sit high
in the woods
on my roof.
Trees sway,
leaves tumble
to ground,
become mulch.
The sun no longer a lemon.
The moon a sliver
of a white thumbnail.
I know where I am.
Where in the dark are you?

Rain

It's midnight
in a downpour
(off and on all spring).

There is a forsaken
beauty about
my little street.

I peer through my window
and realize that
each thing falling
will fall for the last time.

Into the Night

Ignore the world,
        fold it into the moon.

The sphere about to disappear
        into the night, my panther.

I turn on the night light.
Listen to the three flutes.

Nothing will change the heart.
Everything will change the heart.

The conductor is out of sync.

Get the metronome right.
The black eclipse of the heart.

In the Pocket

It's January.
Dark pushes
day aside.

Sometimes we
whisper peculiar
secrets,
tucked away
in the pocket
of my white shirt.

Other times
it would be
better to forget
the grace of
anything—
lose quirky secrets
kept close
under my skin.

Looking through
the window,
I see everyone
who once was
is here now.

Morning Rain

In the suburbs,
on a dark morning
you open the door for
the newspaper, the dog.

Your succulent green robe absorbs
the few drops of rain,
unnoticed as the day begins.

And someday the dark air
will open, make a space in the sky
for us to rest between the raindrops.

Comets

There are black
rocks and dust
hurtling in,
ashes angling
to be ignited.

The dirt ball storm
upsets our sun
and constellations.

The night is filled
with glittery matter.
So much to see;
a cold ball
escaping in the dark
into the show
of stars.

Mother

Most losses add something
nightlight or silence,
a house in hot islands.
We repair to language, the conch
suffocating on the beach.

We talk about anything.
Smart cigarette. Silver lighter.

My father wore a gray hat to the office,
home too chaotic to love.
But he worshipped her nervy synapses,
her darkness a panther,
her lightness a party.
The losses leave

holes, more holes. She pulled
taffy at Christmas.
Jesus meant it to be.
Perfect, ironed sheets,
Sunday lamb dinners
with white folded napkins,
so right.

Vacuuming in your
bathing suit, so wild.
I miss you,
your broken last child.

Pool at 3:00 a.m.

Early morning
in a closed bar
you play alone.
Smells of
scotch, beer,
urine,
the colossal
sadness you
so fear—you need
all of this.

The Ride of Our Lives

Our magic carpet
lifts the leather love seat,
swivel chair.

A spectacle to watch.
Hot air balloons compete.
All our chaotic love—
ante up a coin,
ride the lift, lift the ride.

So Right, So Wild

Gnashing, quarreling,
the wolf is thrown
from its pack.
His fur falls
layers upon layers.

The wolf abandoned,
shifting in
this god-forsaken
suburbia.

In this darkness
his haunting,
terrible howl.
So right so wild.

What Is

Hiked eight miles into a forest
rearranging leaves.

Awesome—

Nightlight touches trees
Oh! Full moon,
a silver dollar.

A far off wolf howls.

Candle

The essential is immaterial—
are you the flicker of white light heat,
or are you the blue flame of the wick?

Tossed Aside

Your tattered clothes,
a purse, a ring, sandals
no longer needed

when you decided
to leave this world—

you left walking,
into a cold river

(no star, no moon
in your dark mind).

Storm

First the power
goes out,
then icy phone
wires crackle.

I dress for sleep
in a parka, a sweater,
heavy pants.

Like obsessions,
tumbling snow
from the evening,
all pettiness
falls away.

Leaves waiting
to come back,
to come back
after a long
snowy separation.

This Is Probably True

All naked I peer ready to dive into that cold dark lake, alone.

A quiet stroke—

Water quenches—

Some say
the more you lay aside,
the more you will forget.

This is probably true.

Daffodils rest on my bed.

Returning

A new robin
nests in an
old tree—
feathers, twigs, mud.

It leaves,
comes back
again,
again,
shifts to
what was before—
leafy greens
and all.

We are the only
ones who can't
come back.

Armadillo

We see an armadillo
lying dirty in its armor
on the road after
a dinner party.

He is so beautiful,
so out of place,
lying under the lights.
A large scaly innocent
with poor vision,
once dug blindly
with sharp claws
for grubs, beetles,
worms.

Bloody and still,
the tough scaly body,
so quiet.

We give him a funeral,
a plastic bag.
Burn it at a pyre.

Provide the wind.
Lift its tail, God.

Night Stars

I slide through the window
one way into heavens—
a sky high, a lovelier place.
Stars I see here have no price,
silver, a more brilliant sliver.
Eventually everyplace dims.

Kate McNairy has been published in *Third Wednesday, Misfits, Chronogram, Many Waters,* and *Echo,* among other magazines. She has also published a chapbook, *June Bug,* from Finishing Line Press in 2014. Kate was a finalist in the Blue Light Poetry Prize and Chapbook Competition in 2013.

She has taken poetry workshops at New York State Summer Writers Institute at Skidmore College where she worked with Henri Cole and Campbell McGrath.

www.ingramcontent.com/pod-product-compliance
Lightning Source LLC
LaVergne TN
LVHW041512070426
835507LV00012B/1518